Study Gu

Printed in the United States of America

First Edition

First Printing, 2017

ISBN-13: 978-1548358952
ISBN-10: 1548358959

www.robertgkroll.com

Dedication

To my father, Tom Kroll, the biggest *Third Man* fan of all.

To the people who give me an inordinate, almost hyperbolic amount of support: Dan, Ma, Jake, Jenny, RJ, Ellen, Tim, Amy, Peter, and Shannon.

Many thanks to Ray Kelly and Wellesnet.

Thanks to John, Phil, and Suzanne for their faith.

This book is dedicated to the memory of Robert Heyl.

About the Author

Robert Kroll is an English professor at St. Clair County Community College and Macomb Community College. He has presented at many conferences on a variety of topics related to Orson Welles, Shakespeare, and more. He was with the Blue Water Film Festival from 2011 to 2014. This is his first book, which is a precursor to a much larger book about Orson Welles' television commercial work.

Table of Contents

Above: Orson Welles in 1941, ten years before *The Lives of Harry Lime.*

Introduction: Welcome to Issue #0

In late 2014, Indiana University announced that they would hold a symposium to commemorate what would have been Orson Welles' 100th birthday in 2015. The symposium would feature academic presentations, speeches from noted scholars, and screenings of Welles' films.

I wanted to be a part of this symposium, but only if I could come up with a unique topic. I eventually settled on the much talked about but rarely explored television commercials Welles worked on towards the end of his life. To my surprise, the proposal was accepted. I figured that my presentation would shed a more positive light on a much-derided era in Welles' life. At best, maybe I would lay the groundwork for other scholars to build on.

The presentation went better than I would have expected. I also realized that the scholar who should build on the presentation is, well, me.

Since that presentation on May 1, 2015 (74 years after the premiere of *Citizen Kane*), I have been working on a book that covers Welles' radio and television commercials. There is more material out there than I would have expected and I have interviewed many people who worked with Welles.

But work on the book can be slow. Many friends and colleagues have asked when the book will be completed. I have to be honest and say that I don't know. Archival materials and interviews have yielded great rewards, but I don't always have access to either. Tracking down materials and interview subjects takes time. At the archives at University of Michigan, I can look at boxes upon boxes of material about *Citizen Kane*, but there are only a couple folders of materials relating to Welles' commercial work. Television commercials don't run end credits like films do, so it takes a lot of detective work to find people to speak with.

Despite the challenges, I am happy with how the work is going. If it takes a decade to finish the project, so be it.

I have given many presentations since that day in 2015, but I am primarily a college English professor. Many students wish to become authors, but do not know what steps they should be taking. I have encouraged self-publishing in the past, but I said so without knowing the first thing about self-publishing.

More students asked about self-publishing during the 2016-2017 school year than any other school year. In one instance, one of my students had already published an autobiography. Another student, Garrett Hadwin, made his short story "Hatched: Prelude" available as an eBook download. Both inspired me to do something with self-publishing. Maybe I can learn something to pass along to aspiring writers that come through my classes.

Around the same time I received the autobiography, news came out the University of Michigan's Screen Arts and Mavericks archives newest acquisition for their Orson Welles collection. The materials came from Beatrice Welles, his youngest daughter. A highlight in the announcement was that the collection includes an entire season's worth of scripts that Welles wrote for a proposed television series based around his character Harry Lime from *The Third Man*.

These TV scripts are of interest to me for many reasons. For one thing, I never knew that Welles had written such a series. I knew he starred in and wrote many episodes for *The Lives of Harry Lime* radio series, but I didn't know there were also television scripts. Additionally, Welles' foray into television in the 1950's is an area I am working on for my larger book project. I studied the script for the proposed TV remake of *Citizen Kane* from the 1950's and written about it for Wellesnet.com. It stands to reason that I will be reading Welles' *Third Man* TV scripts and writing about them for my book.

As anxious as I am to look at those *Third Man* scripts, I realized that I was not as familiar with T*he Lives of Harry Lime* radio series as I could be. I know that Welles adapted portions of the *Harry Lime* episodes he wrote into his film *Mr. Arkadin*, but that was about it. As much as I love *The Mercury Theater on the Air* and Welles' turn in *The Shadow*, I realized I never gave *The Lives of Harry Lime* much of a chance.

I decided that the best way to approach the eventual study of *The Third Man* TV scripts would be to know as much about *The Lives of Harry Lime* radio series as possible.

I bought a couple notebooks and began listening to the series at Internet Archive. I took notes on everything that happened in all 52 episodes, references made in each episode, and anything else I deemed important. I also watched *Mr. Arkadin* for the first time in years to realize fully how much of the radio series was adapted into the film. The goal is to know the entire Harry Lime canon and prepare me for the research when the scripts become available.

That leads to the self-publication of this book.

Having written so much about *The Lives of Harry Lime* for my own purposes, I decided I should send out what I've written into the world. While this study of *The Lives of Harry Lime* came about because of my larger study into Welles' commercial and television work, I feel like this study is its own entity.

The relative simplicity of writing this book also meant that I could learn all about self-publication. Since it is a smaller volume, I could write it relatively quickly and figure out the entire process of publishing my own book. I can confidently tell students more about self-publishing their own works instead of merely suggesting they do so.

While this may essentially be an academic book, I

don't think it is strictly academic. I could write far more in-depth analyses of many episodes, but I am holding out on doing so until I read the *Third Man* TV scripts. I have referred to relevant newspaper articles and Welles films, but not nearly to the extent that I would on other projects. Sections like my attempt at casting a Batman film using Mercury Theater players are flights of fancy inspired by listening to the radio series.

If anything, I consider this book to be two things:

1. A casual, subjective guide to *The Lives of Harry Lime* and its related media.
2. An excuse to learn about self-publishing.

My apologies if this book is not an accurate representation of my academic style or ability. Hopefully you can forgive me for the desire to go a little loose while I work on my larger book project. A lot more work is going into that book. The archival materials and interviews demand far more time. Ultimately, I wanted to produce something of my own and see what I can learn from the experience.

Occasionally, comic book companies will release an "issue #0" of a new or established series. An issue #0 could be a story that takes place outside of the regular monthly continuity. It could be used as a jumping off point to attract new readers to ongoing titles. An Issue #0 could be a soft opening to a series before starting properly with issue #1.

I would like to think of this book in those terms. Welcome to issue #0.

Notes on the Format

– This book is as much of a diary as it is an episode guide. I have broken up parts of the episode guide with other pieces that I wrote and thought about while listening to *The Lives of Harry Lime*. I have also included the dates I listened to each episode.

– The original transmission dates are based on the original airdates by Radio Luxembourg (via the *Lives of Harry Lime* entry at *The Digital Deli Too*). The episodes of *The Lives of Harry Lime* included on the Criterion Collection editions of *The Third Man* and *Mr. Arkadin* follow these dates, so I have elected to follow them as well.

– Every episode entry features a summary along with my own comments about the episode. Other items of interest appear with each entry when applicable. These notes include references to *The Third Man*, references to other works by Orson Welles, choice lines, hints about Harry's past, and other items I feel worth pointing out.

– Many episodes in the series repeat tropes and situations from earlier episodes. As such, comments for those episodes are admittedly not very substantial.

– Due to the age and quality of the episode recordings, many character names are hard to hear and understand. *The Lives of Harry Lime* short story collection allowed many names to be spelled correctly, while others are best guesses.

– This guide is not meant to be the definitive episode guide to *The Lives of Harry Lime*. This is my journey through the series that takes on the format of an episode guide.

The Lives of Harry Lime **Series Credits**

The following credits are applicable to all episodes of *The Lives of Harry Lime*:

Produced by Harry Alan Towers
Directed by Tig Roe
Zither music by Anton Karas
Starring Orson Welles as Harry Lime

Credits are adapted from the opening credits of *The Lives of Harry Lime* and Jonathan Rosenbaum's timeline of Welles' career in *This is Orson Welles* (408).

No other actors besides Orson Welles are credited in any *Harry Lime* episode. Any actors credited in these entries are my own best guesses or come from Rosenbaum's timeline.

Writers are not mentioned in the credits of any *Harry Lime* episodes. The credits included here either come from Rosenbaum's timeline or from the table of contents of the *Lives of Harry Lime* novel published by Pocket Books for *News of the World* in 1952. Graham Greene is not credited as the creator of the Harry Lime character.

The Rosenbaum timeline also notes that, "many of the uncredited programs are scripted by Ernest Borneman." (Welles and Bogdanovich 409) That sentence conceivably covers the credits for episodes that don't have a writer's credit, but the qualifier in the sentence is "many." Since "many…uncredited episodes" does not mean "all uncredited episodes," I have not included Ernest Borneman as the credited writer. This is especially true since I cannot definitively say that Ernest Borneman is the credited writer on an otherwise uncredited episode.

Further, there is dispute as to whether Borneman wrote the episodes Welles is credited for or not. In an interview with series producer Harry Alan Towers, Towers says Borneman came to his office one day seeking payment for episodes of *Harry Lime* that he allegedly wrote. Welles slightly dismissed the notion, pointing out that the scripts weren't very good. ("Reviving Harry Lime" 0:11:51-0:12:30)

Without discounting the claims of Borneman, I have opted to credit Welles for the episodes Rosenbaum credited to Welles. While there is mystery to the authorship of the *Mr. Arkadin* novelization (see entry for "Dead Candidate" on page 44), I cannot definitively say that Borneman wrote any or all of the episodes he claims. Towers didn't specify which episodes Borneman claimed to write in the *Mr. Arkadin* DVD interview, which makes it harder to identify any episodes Borneman claims to have written. This may all change when the Beatrice Welles materials are made available for research at the University of Michigan archives. For now, Welles' credits stay.

Future editions of this book will be updated in light of any further cast and crew credits.

Where to Listen to *The Lives of Harry Lime*

The Lives of Harry Lime is an old time radio show that is in the public domain. As such, all 52 episodes are freely available. More often than not, I listened to the episodes available at the Internet Archive (archive.org). If the quality of the episode too rough, then Old Radio World would have a better recording available. I would also listen to the episodes available on the *Third Man* or *Mr. Arkadin* Criterion Collection DVDs. To me, this helped strengthen the connection between the films and the shows.

The Lives of Harry Lime
Episode 1, "Too Many Crooks"
Written by Orson Welles (Welles and Bogdanovich 408)
Original air date: August 3, 1951
Listened to on April 27, 2017
Source: Internet Archive

Summary: Harry Lime is summoned to Budapest. A man named Fedeke offers him $20,000 to help foil a bank robbery before it actually happens. Tensions between Harry and Fedeke escalate before Harry ultimately decides to become a turncoat.

Choice line: "Poor Shakespeare said a mouthful." - Harry Lime

Comments: Good start to the series. It can be heavy on the exposition at the end, but still a solid piece. Might have been an issue with the audio file but the zither music at the start drowned out a lot of the conversation. Overall theme of the series seems to be how Harry can be a black hat *and* above being arrested. Also, if he is broke by episode four, how much time is between episodes? Was Harry robbed or that easily parted with his money? Also, there is something very English about Harry saying we don't need to the tunnel crew because of their vulgarity.

The Lives of Harry Lime
Episode 2, "See Naples and Live"
Written by Sigmund Miller (Welles, et al 46)
Original transmission: August 10, 1951
Listened to on April 28, 2017
Source: Internet Archive

Summary: Taking place before World War II, Harry is in Italy to dissolve a partnership with a man named Rubio.

While in the country, Harry tries to ply an emerald necklace from a woman named Mrs. Donaldson. Harry takes Donaldson and her assistant Aimee to the ruins of Pompeii to pull off his necklace heist.

Choice line: "I am now the most well-threatened man in Europe, and you have joined an innumerable caravan. *Arrivederci.*" - Harry Lime

Harry's past: Harry is a fluent speaker of Italian. He also has a sister that he has not seen in over a decade due to her disapproval with his profession.

Comments: The use of phenobarbital on the women would be considered rough in any era. In spite of this, this is a very scenic episode within Naples and Pompeii. The chase through the bathhouse is a nice callback to the sewer chase in *The Third Man*, while also foreshadowing a similar chase in Welles' then-upcoming production of *Othello*. A good episode overall, but the phenobarbital use is upsetting.

Above: A street in Pompeii in 2007.

The Lives of Harry Lime
Episode 3, "Clay Pigeon"
Original transmission: August 17, 1951
Listened to on April 28, 2017
Source: Internet Archive

Summary: It is 1942 and Harry is summoned to New York by James Hadley, a man in running for governor of an unnamed state. Pictures that purportedly show Hadley visiting a cathouse have emerged and are being used by a gangster named Kato for bribery. Hadley is willing to pay Lime $15,000 and give a full pardon in "his" state if Harry can get rid of the negatives.

Harry's past: Knows "Lancelot and Elaine" by Alfred, Lord Tennyson by heart.

Potential misidentification: An episode called "New York, 1942" is included among the titles of Harry Lime episodes in Jonathan Rosenbaum's timeline of Welles' career in *This is Orson Welles* (408). Considering the setting for the episode, it is likely that "New York, 1942" is an alternate title for this episode.

Comments: First trip to America in the show, and a very sordid plot. The "identical twin" twist is convenient, but the payoff shows how much of a scoundrel Harry really is. I also have to appreciate that a stray cat comes to visit Harry at the end of the caper.

The Lives of Harry Lime
Episode 4, "A Ticket to Tangier"
Written by Orson Welles (Welles and Bogdanovich 408)
Original transmission: August 24, 1951
Listened to on April 26, 2017
Source: *The Third Man*, Criterion Collection DVD (2007 reissue)

Summary: In Paris and broke, Harry is summoned to Tangier via newspaper ad. Harry was summoned by a woman named Patsy, an air attendant he saw on the flight. Patsy has killed a heroin dealer and wants Harry to help her sell off the heroin. Not wanting to be part of such a trade, Harry does what he can to leave the scene and to prevent the further sale of the heroin.

Choice line: "An awful lot of people can whistle that song." - Harry Lime

Third Man theme: Harry has to whistle "The *Third Man* Theme" in order to get the eponymous ticket to Tangier.

Comments: Solid episode. Plays with elements of *The Third Man* with a far more heroic and altruistic twist. Harry actually comes off as admirable. Can see why this episode was included with the DVD.

The Lives of Harry Lime
Episode 5, "Voodoo"
Original transmission: August 31, 1951
Listened to on April 29, 2017
Source: Internet Archive

Summary: After backing a failed coup at an island near Haiti, Harry goes to Haiti to relax. Harry comes across a man named Sam, who wishes for Harry to steal the Scepter of Henri Christophe from a nearby tribe before an upcoming wedding ceremony. Someone eventually steals the scepter, and Harry must return the scepter to the tribe, lest the married couple be put to death.

Harry's Past: Harry *might* be from Toledo.

Comments: One of the most dastardly plots of the entire series. Tolkan's death is barely mourned, and Harry *still* steals from the tribe and makes *more* money off the deal. The theft of the scepter isn't as crafty as other thefts in the series, but the episode is a stark reminder that Harry is a contemptible man. It is also great to hear Welles' return to Haiti in some fashion after the Federal Theater production of *Macbeth* in 1936.

HEINRICH I.

König von Haiti

Above: 19th century engraving of Henri Christophe by
Austrian artist Blasius Höfel.

Images from the Federal Theater Project's 1936 production of *Macbeth*, directed by Orson Welles. Top, Macbeth with the three witches. Bottom, the final scene.

The Lives of Harry Lime
Episode 6, "The Bohemian Star"
Original transmission: September 7, 1951
Listened to on April 29, 2017
Source: Internet Archive

Summary: London, 1938. A diamond called the Bohemian Star, as big as the Koh-in-Noor, has been recovered by Scotland Yard, which is in London to be replicated for an exhibit of crown jewels from an unnamed South American country. Harry takes the place of Paul Atkinson, an actual Associated Press writer in town with his girlfriend to do a profile on the diamond's owner. But Harry takes on the job in order to steal the Bohemian Star.

Comments: A lighter episode than the last, but almost anything would be a lighter adventure after two people are nearly burned alive. This is also the second time that Lime has made money from accepting awards from the police.

Trivia: Paul allows Harry to take his place as a reporter so that Paul is free to take his girlfriend out that night to see a movie starring Betty Grable and Don Ameche. This might be an error on the writer's part, as Grable and Ameche wouldn't star in a movie until 1940's *Down Argentine Way*, released two years after the events of this episode.

The Lives of Harry Lime
Episode 7, "Love Affair"
Written by Sigmund Miller (Welles, et al 33)
Original transmission: September 14, 1951
Listened to on April 29, 2017
Source: Internet Archive

Summary: Harry is a broker on behalf of Carl Schweig to get the oil rights from the ruler of an unnamed city in Saudi

Arabia. A stranger who is an enemy of Schweig's arrives and tries to get Harry to flip sides.

Comments: This episode was weak. Wasn't totally sure of what was going on with the oil contracts, nor who it was that was against Schweig. By the time the halfway break in the episode came, nothing of any real dramatic value happened. Harry just moved from one place to another without any actual consequence. Didn't really even feel like a Harry Lime story; it was as if he was just around to witness things happen. At least he ended up in Vienna at the end.

The Lives of Harry Lime
Episode 8, "Rogue's Holiday"
Written by Peter Lyon (Welles and Bogdanovich 408)
Original transmission: September 21, 1951
Listened to on April 29, 2017
Source: Internet Archive

Summary: Harry is on a cruise after bilking three Wall Street investors out of $65,000. Harry comes across a woman, Anne, who alleges to be a princess recently run out of an unnamed East German principality. She currently in possession of a pearl necklace that Harry is very interested in. Harry schemes to get the necklace with terrible results.

Choice dialogue:

Harry: I had them priced by a jeweler who said he'd ask £150,000 for them.
Barney: That should keep you in cigarettes for a week or two.

Comments: Now we're back on track. Much better episode this time with a better romance than the last episode. The twist of Harry being "had" is good, and a good deviation to show that Harry can be vulnerable as well. The counterfeit necklace twist feels like a last-minute revision to the script, but was alerted to early enough in the episode to make it work. Overall, a solid episode.

The Lives of Harry Lime
Episode 9, "Work of Art"
Written by Bud Lesser (Welles and Bogdanovich 408)
Original transmission: September 28, 1951
Listened to on April 29, 2017
Source: Internet Archive

Summary: July, 1944. The newspapers of the world are reporting on the death of Hitler. Harry is in Buenos Aires, Argentina. Harry visits Juan Ferendez, an art dealer with dealings in the black market. Ferendez solicits Harry to try and get the favor of Melissa Corday, a woman who runs a very exclusive art gallery. She has a Peter Paul Reubens painting Ferendez is interested in. Ferendez wants Harry to work his way into her personal circle so he can steal the painting from her. Complications arise, culminating the return of the painting. This allows Corday to divorce her husband, who was a Nazi munitions manufacturer.

Comments: A great episode, but I am also a sucker for stories about art theft. Was a little put off that there was another story featuring Harry being "had" again, but it is a worthwhile double cross to be divorced from a Nazi. Also interesting that this episode took place in Argentina after another visit in "The Bohemian Star." I wonder if it was well-known in 1951 that Nazi fugitives were hiding out in Argentina.

The Lives of Harry Lime
Episode 10, "Operation Music Box"
Written by Orson Welles (Welles and Bogdanovich 408)
Original transmission: October 5, 1951
Listened to on April 29, 2017
Source: Internet Archive

Summary: Harry meets Merna Chapwick at an antique store. Chapwick buys a music box for £35 and proceeds to smash it open. Chapwick then offers the shopkeeper money to give the names and addresses of others who had recently purchased similar music boxes. Her Uncle Ian was a politician in Czechoslovakia and left his last will with her before fleeing to America. The only item of note was a music box that might contain emeralds in it, but Chapwick has lost the box. Harry teams up with Merna to find the music box and its contents through whatever means he deems fit.

Theme song: The owner of the music box that ultimately contained the emeralds hated the song the box played, which was "The *Third Man* Theme."

Choice dialogue:

Lime: You're not gonna buy this music box just to smash it up, are you?
Chapwick: Yes, do you mind?
Lime: Alright with me.

Comments: A risky episode considering the multiple acts of sabotage and thievery. Harry loses once again, but this episode has a pressing time element not present in other episodes. This is very much like an early Sherlock Holmes story, which would feature Holmes solving the case, but often too late.

The Lives of Harry Lime
Episode 11, "The Golden Fleece"
Written by Orson Welles (Welles and Bogdanovich 408)
Original transmission: October 12, 1951
Listened to on April 30, 2017
Source: Internet Archive

Summary: Harry is at a bullfight in Spain. He takes on the job of being captain of a yacht to set sail from Algeciras to Hong Kong at the behest of a woman named Nadya. Nadya is the widow of Hans, a captain of the Nazi navy. She eventually reveals to Harry that they have been shipping half a million in gold bars to a General Wai, which turns out to be her father. But Nadya's husband isn't as dead as they thought, and he comes back to get his gold.

Real life: Harry says that the only boat experience he had was when he was on a boat in Lake Winnebago in Wisconsin. Lake Winnebago is about 100 miles north of Kenosha, Wisconsin, Welles' real-life hometown.

Comments: This is an okay episode. Another con gone awry, but a unique twist at the end. Not nearly as good as other recent episodes though. Too much was kept secret and even the return of Hans "from the dead" was easy enough to see coming. Good material, but it never quite takes off.

The Lives of Harry Lime
Episode 12, "Blue Bride"
Original transmission: October 19, 1951
Listened to on May 1, 2017
Source: Internet Archive

Summary: Harry is in an unnamed French coastal town, printing counterfeit money to be shipped by sailors going to French West Africa. A local *commissar* is so intent on capturing Harry that he is neglecting his new wife. Harry finds out the *commissar*'s wife is Sophie Avant, a retired actress. Harry feigns interest in her past and her current relationship to find out about his pursuer. Harry is able to convince Sophie to tell her new husband to go on their honeymoon finally, which should leave Harry in the clear for a major deal, but things go south very quickly.

Choice line: "I have an aversion to French jails." - Harry Lime

Comments: Intro is a bit shaky, and it was convenient that Harry's girl Pauline knew the right people for the plot to work. But this was a great episode for Welles to literally run with. The sense of paranoia runs high in the episode with someone actually on Harry's tail. What is best about the episode is the range in Welles' voice that is used. His voice was always his best asset, and it is used to a great range here. Of course, there is the silver tongue that we're used to but there are louder and more dramatic volumes that come from a very exciting foot chase. The chase itself is beautifully executed, even if the run-ins are also convenient. Harry's alleged aversion to sirens is beautiful though, and the relatively ambiguous ending is great.

The Lives of Harry Lime
Episode 13, "Every Frame has a Silver Lining"
Written by Robert Cenedella (Welles and Bogdanovich 408)
Original transmission: October 26, 1951
Listened to on May 1, 2017
Source: Old Radio World (better sound quality)

Story: Harry is in Tehran for more oil business when a man named Pappas literally runs into him. Pappas is on the run from the police and has $50,000 of opium he hopes Harry can sell. Harry takes the opium, allows Pappas to escape, but helps the police catch Pappas. Harry gets close to a traveling American family so he can present them with a picture that has the opium stuffed inside the frame, thereby turning the family into unwitting smugglers. However, Pappas returns for revenge and takes the family hostage.

Comments: I hated this episode. It was nine episodes ago that Harry pointed out how he isn't a drug dealer and doesn't do it, even if he is a scoundrel. But the thrust of this episode is that Harry wanted to smuggle opium into the United States. The post-script, the sudden turn that the family was a con gang, and putting it all on one of the family members all feels like they had a script from Cenedella that was forced to fit in with the overall series. Events in the series are built on a lot of happenstance that I will accept, but this episode pushed my suspension of disbelief to the limit. I could give the benefit of the doubt that the people who originally heard this could have forgotten about the earlier episode or even missed it, but that is no excuse for a weak story. It might be worse than the earlier "Love Story."

No, this is worse.

The Lives of Harry Lime
Episode 14, "Mexican Hat Trick"
Original transmission: November 2, 1951
Listened to on May 2, 2017
Source: Internet Archive

Summary: Harry is down on his luck in Mexico City and finds out Bruno, a friend of his, has passed away. The messenger who gives this news passes a note to Harry, stating that Bruno murdered someone and blamed another man for it. The note gives instructions on how to prove the man's innocence, but the affidavit papers have been stolen. Despite a busy schedule, Harry says he will eventually investigate the case for 200,000 pesos. Alicia, the innocent man's daughter, eventually joins the case, which leads them to a small town with a vital connection to the murder.

Choice lines: The opening monologue.

Comments: This episode is a great deviation from the norm. Granted, Harry did find a way to get his payment, but the deed here was more altruistic than usual. Some good comedy in this episode as well, with wittier dialogue fueling the funnier moments. The final chase in the church has a Hitchcockian feel to it. Overall, a great chance to see Harry as a detective instead of a confidence man.

The Lives of Harry Lime
Episode 15, "Art is Long and Lime is Fleeting"
Written by Sigmund Miller (Welles, et al 22)
Original transmission: November 9, 1951
Listened to on May 3, 2017
Source: Internet Archive

Summary: Harry meets two women, Inez and Aurora, in Paris and passes himself off as a rare art dealer. He pays

12,000 francs for a painting of a bather that he thinks he can pass off as a Renoir. Harry is then able to get the painting priced at 4 million francs. Unfortunately, Harry runs into Paul Bazin, a man he has ripped off in the past. Harry promises that he will cut Bazin in on the art deal he is about to make. After some negotiations and stalling, a Renoir expert from the Louvre arrives to verify the painting, which could be worth 20 million francs if real. Bazin steals it, and a chase ensues. Harry gets the painting back, but tosses it into a vagrant's fire to prevent its identification. The expert wasn't fooled by the painting, but won't report Harry's scheme in the hopes that Harry has learned his lesson.

Choice line: "Mr. Lime, if I had everyone arrested who tries to sell a fake picture, the prisons of Paris would be full." - Bordet, the Renoir expert

Comments: Very good episode. The up sell on the painting was the perfect way to get Bazin to cool off a little and we have a great foot chase once again. Excellent way to get rid of the painting.

Bordet's final scene is noteworthy, as it is a precursor to tropes in Welles' *F for Fake*, such as this exchange featuring Clifford Irving:

> Irving: You're a painter. Why do you want people to do fakes?
> (Girl): (*laughing*) Because the fakes are good as the real ones and there's a market and there's a demand.

> *Cut to:*

> Irving: If you didn't have an art market, then fakers could not exist. (*F for Fake* 0:20:41)

24

Harry must have learned his lesson, as there are no episodes featuring art theft after this episode.

Alternate ending: "Art is Long and Lime is Fleeting" ends on a different note in the 1952 *Lives of Harry Lime* short story collection. There, Bordet confirms that the painting is an authentic Renoir, which Lime says "disturbed me for many days." (Miller 31) The stories in the *Harry Lime* collection run around 10 pages each, so this alternate ending allows "Art is Long..." to be consistent with lengths of the other stories.

The Lives of Harry Lime
Episode 16, "In Pursuit of a Ghost"
Original transmission: November 16, 1951
Listened to on May 7, 2017
Source: Internet Archive

Summary: It is the Fall of 1945 and Harry is in an unnamed South American country. Harry is pulled into the world of General Valdez, who is attempting to take over the unnamed country with the assistance of an American gangster only known as El Zorro. Harry spins a tale saying that El Zorro has left town. Valdez believes the story even when Harry confesses he made it up. Harry tries to flee, but is forced into retrieving El Zorro.

Comments: Interesting episode, but the pace felt too rushed. The plot was very convoluted, with the "ghost" Harry was chasing to be a lazy attempt at gaslighting him. "Dead Candidate" (episode 29) handles similar themes much better.

The Lives of Harry Lime
Episode 17, "Horseplay"
Written by Peter Lyon (Welles and Bogdanovich 408)
Original transmission: November 23, 1951
Listened to on May 8, 2017
Source: Internet Archive

Summary: Back in Paris. Harry and his compatriot Andre are in a bar and attempt a con. Andre talks to a man in the bar's corner and drops a wallet that contains a lot of information about horse racing. The man returns the wallet to Harry, the owner of the wallet. Harry lets the man in on the races that he is betting on and lets it slip that he is fixing the races. The man wants in, and Harry sets up an elaborate betting parlor to bilk the man out of his money.

Real-life connection: Lime offers Perrier water in his hotel room. Welles would eventually become the voice of Perrier water for a series of advertisements in the seventies.

Have I heard this before?: Yes, as this is basically the plot of *The Sting*, right down to how the bet is *placed*.

Comments: I admit I had a hard time keeping up with this one, which I suppose is the point of it all. However, the amount of money seemed to keep fluctuating along with unclear exchange rates. Then again, I'm not much of a gambler, so my interest was minimal during this episode.

The Lives of Harry Lime
Episode 18, "Three Farthings for Your Thoughts"
Original transmission: November 20, 1951
Listened to on May 11, 2017
Source: Internet Archive

Summary: Harry is at a pub in Liverpool when he sees a

woman hold up the publican. Oddly enough, she only wants the coins. Harry recognizes her as Helen, the wife of Bill, who just went to prison for a bank robbery. Helen is looking for three farthings that are scratched in a way that give the address to a house where £20,000 is hidden. Bill managed to escape from prison, but is killed by his former partner Baxter. Harry gets to the address scratched on two of the farthings, only to be confronted by Baxter and his accomplice, also looking for the £20,000.

Theme song: Harry hums "The *Third Man* Theme" while breaking into the abandoned house that has the £20,000.

Comments: A good fight scene at the end and a clever code hidden in the coins, but a bit of a bust overall. Interesting concept, but it sputtered out quickly. For whatever reason, I just feel ambivalent about this episode.

The Lives of Harry Lime
Episode 19, "The Third Woman"
Original transmission: December 7, 1951
Listened to on May 12, 2017
Source: Internet Archive

Summary: *Corporal* Lime is in Lisbon during World War II. He is asked by his superiors to be a spy on behalf of the British to infiltrate an underground German factory and stop the new rocket weapon that the Nazis are manufacturing. The original spy they sent in has been kidnapped and Harry is tasked with rescuing them.

Choice line: "Sorry I only got you in the leg, old man, but I never was much of a shot." - Harry Lime

Harry's Past: Harry served in the Army in World War II and was stationed in London. He was running contraband while serving and was smuggling while serving in Marseilles in 1937.

Comments: Good episode. There is a visceral quality to this one, as I am sure everyone involved in the series wanted to sink their teeth into the Nazis. There was a lot of extra flair in Welles' voice when he was shooting the Nazi's leg and hand in order to get the information he needed. But the ending did feel like a cop out. I'm glad that the girl was saved, but the finding out that Harry's info was useless was a little annoying. They could have framed the episode as a rescue if that was the real plot; although, the higher-ups were annoyed with Harry enough that it may have been worth being a thorn in their side. Overall, a timely, well-made episode that added nicely to Harry's back story.

The Lives of Harry Lime
Episode 20, "An Old Moorish Custom"
Written by Irvan Ashkinazy (Welles and Bogdanovich 408)
Original transmission: December 14, 1951
Listened to on May 13, 2017
Source: Internet Archive

Summary: In Algiers, Harry befriends a woman named Valarie. Valarie is a descendant of the pirate Barbarossa. Harry is mainly in Algiers to get money for El Sikkeena, a Bedouin gangster. Harry is questioned by a detective about someone El Sikkeena knows that goes by the name Pierre DuBois. DuBois and El Sikkeena are after the buried treasure of Barbarossa, valued at over a billion francs. Harry tries to warn Valarie's grandfather Armand D'Aronj, who possesses the map to Barbarossa's treasure. Armand will not speak with Harry at all, as the police stopped by and warned that Harry is a bad man. Harry says he will foil the plot in exchange for a percentage of the treasure. A firefight ensues, but only stops when D'Aronj gives up the map. Harry leads the men to the treasure, and potentially a trap.

Choice line: "No need to worry, honey, I'm like a pair of socks: neither right nor left." - Harry Lime

Comments: Great episode. With the scheme slowly revealed in the guise of a love story and a great battle to boot, this episode steered away from the more grievous hand-waving twists that became too common in the series. It actually sounded like Harry was done for at the end of the episode. And seriously, what good is a story about pirates if there isn't a firefight on a beach? As for romance, Harry even seems heartbroken when he loses Valarie at the end of the episode. One of my favorites from the series.

AROUDÌ,

Above: Illustration of Oruç Reis, aka Barbarossa, by Charles-Etienne Motte (modeled after a drawing by Achille Deveria).

Les musulmans, armés de tout ce qui leur tombe sous la main, fondent sur les chrétiens.

Above: 1869 illustration by Charles Farine of Oruç Reis (Barbarossa) capturing a galley.

The Lives of Harry Lime
Episode 21, "It's a Knockout"
Original transmission: December 21, 1951
Listened to on May 14, 2017
Source: Internet Archive

Summary: In Havana, Harry and his compatriot Jenny are trying to con a man named Stan Pierce out of $30,000. Harry and Jenny claim that they have been sponsoring fights for Poncho Calados, who they claim is a boxer on the rise. They set up an illegal, unsanctioned match that they can fix in order to relieve Pierce of his money.

Choice line: "I always find it refreshing to relieve a rich sucker of money when he thinks he's gotta steal from someone else." - Harry Lime

Comments: A good episode, if stifled by the fact that the twist at the end is easy to predict.

The Lives of Harry Lime
Episode 22, "Two is Company"
Written by Orson Welles (Welles and Bogdanovich 408)
Original transmission: December 28, 1951
Listened to on May 15, 2017
Source: Internet Archive

Summary: While in Sicily, Harry gets caught up in the matters of competing American grocery store chains. Gus Schmidt, the head of Schmidt's Luxury Markets, is smitten with Emily Hickenlooper, heiress of the Hickenlooper grocery empire. The Hickenloopers and Schmidts have gathered to discuss a merger, which Emily is against. Harry plays his version of matchmaker, conscripting Sicilian bandit Barznini into a plot where Gus and Emily both think the other has been kidnapped. Harry twists the situation enough that he should be able to walk away from the incident with $36,500 for his assistance in rescuing either of them.

Coincidence: Two of the characters in this episode are named "Hickenlooper." Coincidentally, Welles' screenplay *The Big Brass Ring* would be adapted by George Hickenlooper into a short film in 1997 and a feature length film in 1999.

Welles' influence: Lime and Schmidt drink negronis at the start, which is why Schmidt is so hungover the next day. Welles is partially responsible for the negroni becoming well-known in the United States. Welles stated his fondness for the drink in December 1947 while making *Black Magic* in Sicily, saying, "The bitters are excellent for your liver, the gin is bad for you. They balance each other." (Erskine)

Choice line: "In a love affair, I mean a real romance, two is company, and the third man is a crowd." - Harry Lime

Comments: The plot to get the money out of a Capulet v. Montague scenario is perfect for the series. Easy enough episode to follow with no inexplicable twists or ridiculous moralizing. Welles clearly has the best handle on writing for the character. Harry's loss is another great way to highlight how he can lose and still be suave in the entire process.

The Lives of Harry Lime
Episode 23, "Cherchez la Gem"
Original transmission: January 4, 1952
Listened to on May 15, 2017
Source: Internet Archive

Summary: On a boat from China, Harry finds an arguing

couple and becomes smitten with the woman. Harry finds out her name is Anne, and he takes her for drinks to ease her seasickness. Anne reveals that the man, Joe, is her husband. Joe has recently finished serving five years in jail for the theft of $75,000 worth of jewels. Joe's partner Jameson managed to get away with the crime and is currently living in Honolulu. Joe and Anne intend on getting the $75,000 worth of jewels back. In Hawaii, Harry also becomes smitten with Moana, who works at a hotel that is close to where Jameson lives. Harry tries to work the romance with Moana in order to get to the jewels.

Choice dialogue:

Joe: I'm Joe Brissi, the husband of the babe you got tight with on the boat.
Harry: It's a habit of mine to get tight with wives. Which husband are you? I mean, which wife was yours?

Comments: Solid writing at the first half, but this one fell apart toward the end. Moana was too fragile and lilting to be an effective character. While I'm glad Harry finally addressed his womanizing, the episode didn't wrap up in a way that lives up to its first half; the dialogue toward the end even sounded like they were trying to fill out the episode's allotted time.

The Lives of Harry Lime
Episode 24, "Hand of Glory"
Written by Jonquil Anthony (Welles, et al 97)
Original transmission: January 11, 1952
Listened to on May 18, 2017
Source: Internet Archive

Summary: Feeling Paris on a boat for England, Harry chats up Helen, who invites him to her little town Fallowmire.

Harry decides to stay at the house of Helen's uncles, Mr. Gregory and Mr. John. Harry finds out that they are alchemists who wish to open a school for alchemy. But Harry becomes aware that he is a guest at the house only to become part of a sacrifice to attain alchemical knowledge.

Potential misidentification: Jonathan Rosenbaum's timeline of Welles' career lists an episode called "The Secret of Making Gold" in the *Lives of Harry Lime* section (408). With Gregory and John attempting to become alchemists through supernatural means, "The Secret of Making Gold" is likely an alternate title used in syndication.

Comments: I'm positive this episode started with a chase in order to make the story seem more exciting, as this is one of the weakest episodes yet. An already thin plot was stretched even thinner. Even worse, the potentially interesting plot point of the town being haunted is abandoned as quickly as it is brought up. The dialogue from the brothers was exceptionally annoying. Bad voices and awful, spill-all-the-beans dialogue undercuts what little menace that may have had. The episode sounds like it was originally intended to be a *Hound of the Baskervilles*-type story, but was forced into being a *Harry Lime* episode. This was a bad episode in every conceivable way.

The Lives of Harry Lime
Episode 25, "Double Double Cross"
Original transmission: January 18, 1952
Listened to on May 19, 2017
Source: Internet Archive

Summary: Monte Carlo, 1936. At a casino, Harry makes a move for Louise, but her husband Pierre comes along before he can make any major moves. A disagreement is cut short when they find out he is *the* Harry Lime. Pierre and Louise convince Harry to join a scheme of theirs, which involves Harry skydiving into England to smuggle in American money. The scheme works for some time, but when Louise's true feelings for Harry become known, Pierre finds a way to get rid of Harry for good.

Choice line: "To a successful gambler, mademoiselle, the word 'prudent' doesn't exist." - Harry Lime

Comments: This episode dragged in a few parts, but the double double cross of the title was nicely executed. The skydiving element really added another dimension to the standard schemes of the series. This episode may also feature the longest time span for events to unwind. Overall a solid episode with a very satisfying twist that actually delivered on its set-up instead of resorting to hand-waving make it work.

The Lives of Harry Lime
Episode 26, "Five Thousand Pengoes and a Kiss"
Written by Carl Jampel (Welles, et al 82)
Original transmission: January 25, 1952
Listened to on May 19, 2017
Source: Internet Archive

Summary: Post-war Budapest. Harry runs into Helene, a show business woman he knows. Helene wishes to leave the country, but her emigration papers are not going through. The government hopes that by keeping Helene in Hungary, her fugitive husband will inevitably return to her and can be arrested. Harry charges her 5,000 gold pengoes to try and get her out of the country.

History: While no year is mentioned, this story had to have taken place when the pengoe still had some value. It is hard to believe this is a post-war story, as the pengoe was replaced in 1946.

Comments: Good, but not a specifically great episode.

The Lives of Harry Lime
Episode 27, "Dark Enchantress"
Original transmission: February 1, 1952
Listened to on May 21, 2017
Source: Internet Archive

Summary: Harry is spending his time in a rough bar in Algiers with a woman named Magda. He then meets a young woman from San Francisco named Susan, who is interested in seeing Magda sing. Susan is a free spirit who is wandering around a lot of sketchy places in town at the consternation of her parents, who have a detective named Claremont following her around. After visiting a man named Charles at the behest of Magda. Harry finds Susan the next day in a daze. At a convent, away from the prying eyes of Claremont, Harry discovers that Charles drugged Susan before releasing her. Charles orders Susan's well-connected parents to pay a ransom of 5,000 francs or he will reveal that Susan was spending time with him. Working out the transfer of money, Harry discovers Magda and Charles are the same person. Because of his help, Harry is given the ransom money as a reward. Harry then donates it to the convent.

Choice line: "I'm a surprising kind of guy. I swore a solemn oath years ago never to do anything fundamentally decent if I could possibly avoid it, and look what I'm up to now!" - Harry Lime

Comments: Good episode featuring an altruistic Harry. My only complaint is the disguise of Magda as Charles, as the same tone of voice was used for both, which made the twist a little confusing and uninteresting. Radio actors can usually pull off many extra voices, so it is odd that the Magda/Charles actress elected to (or was directed to) maintain the same voice for both parts. Something was certainly fishy, but even a deeper tone in her voice would have helped make the actual revelation shocking. I suppose it was a good subtle clue to the audience, but considering Welles' own vocal dexterity, I'm surprised something like this wasn't pushed for.

Interlude:

Batman, starring the Mercury Players

I believe that Orson Welles could have made a great Batman film.

Admittedly, such an idea has its basis in a hoax; however, I thought about this hypothetical film as I made my way through *The Lives of Harry Lime.* The seedy characters and morally questionable situations of the series are further proof (to me, at least) that Welles could have pulled off such a film. Listening to "Dark Enchantress" was the catalyst to elaborate fully on the idea, but the idea has been in my mind for a long time.

On May 2, 2015, I attended a screening of Orson Welles' *Too Much Johnson*. Thought to be lost, the film was restored in 2013. An edited 30 minute version was created from the surviving footage, but at the screening we were treated to the full hour of surviving footage.

While *Too Much Johnson* revolves around Joseph Cotton's character eluding his mistress' husband, Cotten is shown running and jumping across rooftops. Since we were able to watch relatively unedited rushes of the film, we were able to see Cotten very precariously dangle off of a roof edge, come back to the roof, only to dangle again for the next shot. The audience was gasping audibly and frequently. Cotten risked his life six decades before special effects could erase wire work and allow actors to do similar stunts safely.

As I watched the footage, I had to think back to a hoax pulled by comic book writer Mark Millar. In a 2003 column for Comic Book Resources, Millar claimed that someone had found a sketch Orson Welles had done as part of a Batman film he wanted to make. Of course, it wasn't true; artist Bryan Hitch was responsible for the drawing that Millar passed off as a Welles. I didn't come across the hoax until 2005, so I wasn't able to be shocked at the revelation.

After the *Too Much Johnson* screening, with the Millar article and the new daredevil side of Joseph Cotten running in my mind, I began thinking about how Welles would have done an excellent job with a Batman film. *The Lives of Harry Lime* further confirmed my thoughts.

In the mid-nineties, the comic book news magazine *Wizard* had a regular feature titled "Casting Call." Every month, "Casting Call" would feature the cast of a popular comic book and an actor or actress the writers thought would play the role well. The column was a welcome dose of speculation in the years before comic book adaptations became ubiquitous in theaters.

In the tradition of "Casting Call," I present my wholly speculative version of *Batman* featuring the Mercury Players. To figure out the best group of actors and characters to draw from, I set the time range from 1939 to 1942. This period covers the first appearance of Batman in 1939 and goes to the release of *The Magnificent Ambersons* in 1942. This range also creates a more manageable list of Batman characters to work with.

By no means would a feature contain every single one of these characters. This cast list is meant to be a stable of actors and characters to draw from, not a specific suggestion for a story.

As much as I enjoy the Millar/Hitch hoax, I know for a fact that I wouldn't be fooled by it now. I've handled many of Welles' own drawings and paintings and I am very familiar with Bryan Hitch's style.

But I like to speculate on what could have been.

Above: Screenshots of Joseph Cotten hanging off of and standing on a rooftop in the workprint for *Too Much Johnson*.

The Cast:

Joseph Cotten as Batman/Bruce Wayne
- – Cotten was handsome enough to be Bruce Wayne. He wore a suit well and he had a great smile. Cotton's jawline would have looked great in the cowl. The stunts from *Too Much Johnson* are proof that he would have been more than capable for the part.

Orson Welles as The Joker
- – I think that Welles could channel the righteous rage shown during *Citizen Kane*'s Madison Square Garden speech into an absolutely devilish Joker. Since The Joker's first ever threats were made over the radio, Welles would have been perfect for the role.

Tim Holt as Robin/Dick Grayson
- – Why not? George Amberson was rambunctious and impulsive. Put Holt in a domino mask and he would have been perfect as Batman's sidekick.

Dorothy Comingore as Catwoman/Selena Kyle
- – Susan Alexander's personality during the final years of her marriage to Charles Foster Kane would be appropriate Catwoman. Comingore's own abilities as a dancer would have made her perfect as Catwoman.

Agnes Moorehead as Martha Wayne
- – I am hesitant to cast her as another mother in a Welles production, but because of her dress during the *Citizen Kane* trailer, I can't stop imagining her otherwise. It just works for me.

Everett Sloane as Thomas Wayne
- Much like Agnes Moorehead, I see Sloane in the *Citizen Kane* trailer and I see Thomas Wayne.

Ray Collins as Alfred Stryker
- Alfred Stryker was the first Batman antagonist in Detective Comics #27. Sure Collins was an antagonist in *Citizen Kane*, but he is stocky enough for the role and able to give the role the necessary evil it requires.

Erskine Sanford as Commissioner Gordon
- Sanford is commanding enough a presence that he would have been a great foil for Batman.

Paul Stewart as Dr. Hugo Strange
- Granted, he would have had to shave his head or wear a bald cap, but Steward has the right look for one of Batman's earliest antagonists

George Coulouris as Alfred Pennyworth
- As Bruce Wayne's personal butler, Coulouris would have brought calm to the tortured world of Batman.

The Lives of Harry Lime
Episode 28, "Earl on Troubled Waters"
Original transmission: February 8, 2017
Listened to on May 26, 2017
Source: Internet Archive

Summary: In London, Harry is speaking with an acquaintance named Robinson, who is trying to get Harry to smuggle the $30,000 he just stole out of the country. Robinson also thinks that Harry can't possibly live up to the reputation he's created. To this end, Robinson bets Harry that he can't convince an American couple that he is British and get the $30,000 out of the country. Harry befriends a Texan couple who are willing to help him out. This might work out, but there is a pesky child who keeps getting into Harry's business.

Harry's past: Harry's father was Irish.

Comments: Not a great episode, but an interesting foray into a, for lack of a better term, adorable plot.

The Lives of Harry Lime
Episode 29, "Dead Candidate"
Written by Orson Welles (Welles and Bogdanovich 408)
Original transmission: February 15, 1952
Listened to on May 26, 2017
Source: Internet Archive

Summary: Harry is on a boat to a fictional South American country to, ostensibly, endorse the sale of Buzzo cola to the island. But Harry gets mixed up in the politics of the country. The current regime, headed up by a General, ousted Campeau, the more popular leader of the country in a coup. In order to maintain rule over the country and appear more democratic to the outside world, Joachimo, a diplomat for the country, suggests holding an election. Joachimo further suggests that the General is put up for election against Campeau, who is believed to have died in the coup. Risky as it sounds, the election goes ahead with the General against a dead man. The election does not go as smoothly as expected, and the country's preference for Freezo cola may play a part in the results.

Shakespeare: Joachimo says that they will "busy giddy minds," a reference to *Henry IV Part 2*, Act IV, Scene III.

Choice line: "The voting public is notoriously ungrateful." - Joachimo

Misidentification: This and "Buzzo Gospel" are listed as separate episodes in Jonathan Rosenbaum's timeline in *This is Orson Welles* (408). They are the same episode, but the alternate title is likely from a different syndicated version.

Post-series: Welles adapted "Dead Candidate" into a full screenplay with the new title *V.I.P.* for Alexander Korda. Korda passed, and it was further re-written as a novel titled *Une Grosse Legume* by Maurice Bessey. This is one of possibly two Welles adaptations by Bessey, as he may or may not have written the novelization for *Mr. Arkadin*.

Comments: I can see why Welles would want to turn this episode into a feature film. As short as this episode is, it does not feel rushed. The political maneuvering is done with great economy. It is possible to add in a lot more should a feature have been made. The whole episode is a screed against a dictatorship while also taking a few cracks at American politics in the process, all while Harry sits back and watches it all go down.

The Lives of Harry Lime
Episode 30, "It's in the Bag"
Written by Orson Welles (Welles and Bogdanovich 408)
Original transmission: February 15, 1952
Listened to on May 27, 2017
Source: Internet Archive

Summary: Harry is on the Orient Express from Istanbul to Belgrade via the Balkans. No matter how annoyed Harry gets of his compartment companion Stathacopoulos, Harry is sticking around to try and relieve Stathacopoulos of his $10,000. Stathacopoulos is a black marketeer and wants to partner up with Harry upon discovering that Harry is a counterfeiter. Harry agrees, but he maneuvers the deal so that Stathacopoulos is arrested as a counterfeiter at their next train stop. Another group boards the train after the arrest and takes the same compartment as Harry. This new group begins a scheme of their own as the train moves through the mountains.

Choice line: "The wine of his country, although tasting like concentrated extract of candy store with a bit of cough medicine thrown in, had the kick of a proverbial army mule." - Harry Lime

Comments: Welles really seems to want sound to carry the story's intensity. This episode is a later, yet indirect application of techniques refined in the *Mercury Theater on the Air* production of *The War of the Worlds.* The tunnel chase echoes the final chase in *The Third Man* (almost literally) and the Agatha Christie influence is obvious. Welles' potential love of pulps is present here and in full effect.

The Lives of Harry Lime
Episode 31, "Hyacinth Patrol"
Written by Virginia Cooke (Welles, et al 109)
Original transmission: February 29, 1952
Listened to on May 28, 2017
Source: Internet Archive

Summary: Harry is at a disreputable bar in Cristobal, near the Panama Canal. He gets in between two men, Tiger Dolan and Ross Nugent. Dolan is an ex-boxer and member of the Hyacinth Patrol, a group that clears hyacinths from the Panama Canal to control the mosquito population. Dolan is smitten with Nugent's girlfriend Lola. Nugent is hot-headed, demanding the bartender to throw out Harry just for looking at Lola. Dolan tells Harry that he can prove that Nugent is a traitor to America and asks Harry for help in proving his accusations.

Comments: As the middle portion of the story began to drag, I was in agreement with Harry that the story might not be worth our time. But the plot that Nugent finally came up with was one that worked and had solid imagery. One thing that did get annoying was Dolan's romantic entanglements. Dolan is fond of many women and Harry describes them all in excess. Good episode, but it easily bogs down. I admit that I may also be spoiled after back-to-back episodes written by Welles.

The Lives of Harry Lime
Episode 32, "Turnabout is Foul Play"
Original transmission: March 7, 1952
Listened to on May 28, 2017
Source: Internet Archive

Summary: Nazi profiteer Hans Kroft attempts to woo a British U.N. Representative named Manheim into letting him become involved in post-war European industrialization. Kroft needs Harry's assistance, so he sends his daughter Freida try to woo Harry. Harry eventually attempts to broker a deal between all parties in order to steal £30,000 from the negotiations.

Comments: The episode took a while to get going and the ending was rather predictable. Typing up the episode summary based on my notes was rough, as the events of the episode seemed ineffectual, no matter how heavy they would have been in real life. Combine that with a bizarre post-script and an episode with good intentions fell flat.

The Lives of Harry Lime
Episode 33, "Violets, Sweet Violets"
Original transmission: March 14, 1952
Listened to on May 29, 2017
Source: Internet Archive

Summary: Back to Marseilles. Col. Van Goethe of the German occupational police knows Harry's reputation and tells Harry that he is officially under watch. But Harry has been able to lure Annie, an elderly street vendor of violets, into his newest scheme. Violets sold by Annie are a pass to buy black market items from Harry and a man named Grippo. Of course, things don't go according to plan.

Comments: Good scheme and great visuals, but the action behind everything was vague enough that I lost interest after a while. By the time of the first break, about the only thing that happened of any consequence was that Harry got in contact with Grippo. I understand keeping unsavory elements to a minimum in order to appeal to a broader audience, but it was easy to lose interest in what was happening.

The Lives of Harry Lime
Episode 34, "Faith, Lime, and Charity"
Original transmission: March 21, 1952
Listened to on May 30, 2017
Source: Internet Archive

Summary: On the way to Agra, India, Harry is sharing a train car with a Mrs. Hadley. Hadley needs £3,000 to refurbish an orphanage that she lost in a fire. Hadley could ask for help from her friend Lady Edith Bannon Murdock, but is too afraid to ask. Harry is all for helping. Harry gets in contact with Lady Edith and asks for £5,000 (with £2,000 to go to him). After a visit to the Taj Mahal, Harry's relationship with Lady Edith begins to blossom. Harry is struck with the news that Mrs. Hadley may not be as altruistic as she claims.

Potential misidentification: Jonathan Rosenbaum's timeline in *This is Orson Welles* lists an episode called "Little One" in the *Lives of Harry Lime* section (408). Considering Hadley's nickname in this episode is "Little One," it is safe to say that "Little One" is an alternate title for this episode.

Comments: Great episode. The conceit is definitely meant to play on (or balance out) how evil it was of Harry to steal the penicillin in *The Third Man*. But the con was a solid and worked nicely. Some of the romancing is standard, if hyperbolic at this point (*every* woman Harry meets is the most beautiful in the world) and every antagonist has a secret identity, but the plot worked within the standard tropes.

The Lives of Harry Lime
Episode 35, "Pleasure before Business"
Original transmission: March 28, 1952
Listened to on May 31, 2017
Source: Internet Archive

Summary: Post-war Venice. Harry lures his friend Joan Willoughby into stealing jewels from Count Della Rubia, someone Harry has been working for the previous three weeks. Joan is to feign a relationship with the count so Harry can steal the jewels. Things get complicated when Joan actually begins to fall for the count.

Cast: It sounds like Robert Arden plays Rico.

Comments: Nothing special about this episode. Jewels are a fine enough MacGuffin, but nothing about this episode particularly stood out.

The Lives of Harry Lime
Episode 36, "Fool's Gold"
Original transmission: April 4, 1952
Listened to on June 1, 2017
Source: Internet Archive

Summary: Back in Paris. Harry is asked to smuggle some gold and heads to Beirut. He meets up with smugglers Clancy and Sing for this outing. A shipment of gold is coming in for a Sheikh who is the biggest gold dealer in Beirut. Harry tries to get close to the Sheikh under the alias of Dr. Lime, archaeologist. As usual, things do not go according to plan.

Comments: Below average. Plots like this are repetitive at this point, especially after the previous episode. Falura is not a very well-rounded character. The Sheikh isn't very good either, as he is easily fooled by Harry's attempt to leave the palace.

Despite these flaws, I do enjoy the conversational aspect of the series. The manner in which Harry tells his tales evokes how Welles was in real life. It is like having a dinner with Harry Lime at Ma Maison.

The Lives of Harry Lime
Episode 37, "Man of Mystery"
Written by Orson Welles
Original transmission: April 11, 1952
Listened to on June 2, 2017
Source: Internet Archive

Summary: Vienna, (potentially) 1947. Harry is summoned by a Mr. Arkadian for a special job. Arkadian claims that he wants to construct airfields in Portugal, but is allegedly worried about compromising information that could prevent him from doing so. Because Arkadian also alleges that amnesia has taken away all memory prior to 1927, he tasks Harry with creating an "intelligence check" into Arkadian's past. But the people who know about Arkadian are turning up dead shortly after Harry interviews them.

Cast: Frédéric O'Brady as Gregory Arkadian. (Welles and Bogdanovich 408) O'Brady would go on to play Oscar in *Mr. Arkadin.*

Choice line: "Mr. Lime, I'm not hiring your so easily adjustable conscience. I'm buying your knowledge of the continental underworld." – Mr. Gregory Arkadian

Comments: Indeed, this is *Mr. Arkadin* in about 30 minutes. Most of the characters are here. The story even starts out with an empty plane in mid-flight. Even as a half hour piece, the story still worked. A shorter run-time for the story arguably forces Arkadian to be more sinister. The cinematic Arkadin's presence is felt everywhere in the film, but the radio Arkadian is more vicious about eliminating his past.

Above: Frédéric O'Brady (credited just as O'Brady in the film) in the trailer for *Mr. Arkadin*. O'Brady originated the role of Mr. Arkadin in "Man of Mystery," with the name originally as "Arkadian."

Following page: Robert Arden in the trailer for *Mr. Arkadin*. Arden acted in many episodes of *The Lives of Harry Lime*.

Mr. Arkadin
Version: The "Corinth" version
Source: The Complete *Mr. Arkadin*, **Criterion**
Collection DVD
Written and directed by Orson Welles
Starring: Akim Tamiroff, Gregoire Aslan, Patricia
Medina, Jack Watling, Orson Welles, Mischa Auer,
Peter van Eyck, Michael Redgrave, Suzanne Flon,
O'Brady, Katina Pasinou, Tamera Shane, Paola Mori,
Robert Arden
Viewed: June 14, 2017

Story: Guy Van Stratten, a black marketeer and smuggler
of cigarettes, is about to leave Italy when he is visited by a
man seconds away from dying. Van Stratten is given two
names, one of which is "Arkadin." Van Stratten sets out to
find Gregory Arkadin by getting close to his daughter,
Raina. Van Stratten eventually meets Gregory Arkadin at a
party. Arkadin tasks Van Stratten with investigating his
own past. Arkadin claims that he has amnesia and has
forgotten the last 20 years of his life. Arkadin ostensibly
hopes that Van Stratten can fill in the blanks, but Arkadin's
motives are far more sinister than he lets on.

The Lives of Harry Lime
Episode 38, "The Painted Smile"
Original transmission: April 18, 1952
Listened to on June 16, 2017
Source: Internet Archive

Summary: Harry is on vacation in Taormina, Sicily. He is invited to a traveling circus by his friend Tony, who performs in the circus as a clown who performs with tigers. Tony is smitten with Nola, another member of the circus, but she is totally uninterested. After the circus, Harry is visited by Tony's daughter, Therese, who is trying to track down her father. She is unaware of her father's profession, which is exactly what Tony wants, as he is too embarrassed to let her know. Tony reveals to Harry that Therese is also unaware of his real job as an emerald smuggler. As such, Tony wants Harry to give Therese the fortune he has been saving up for her when she turns 21, should he be unable to do it himself. Therese eventually finds out about her father's circus profession and joins Harry for a show later in the night, only to witness tragedy.

Comments: Great episode. Harry really takes the back seat here and Tony's arc is one of the strongest in the series. The layers of sound in this one make it seem like Harry is giving a direct address to the audience, breaking the fourth wall in a flashback. Is Harry a meta-ghost, speaking of past events as they happen in the past tense? Before I go too deep into nonsense, this is a fine story.

The Lives of Harry Lime
Episode 39, "Harry Joins the Circus"
Original transmission: April 25, 1952
Listened to on June 18, 2017
Source: Internet Archive

Summary: Harry is in Rome when he visits Sir Evan, a UN representative from England. Harry shows Sir Evan a photograph purportedly of Hans Hessel, who was allegedly Adolph Hitler's personal secretary. Sir Evan eventually confirms the man's identity, as he had dealt with Hessel during the war. The episode flashes back to Harry's time in a circus. Harry has become friends with Louisa, an 18-year-old trapeze artist in the circus. Louisa is in the circus in order to track down Hans Hessel, who would use the circus in unsuspecting towns to distract children while the Nazis would abduct the parents. Speaking with a clown named "Geeko," Harry begins to realize that the clown may actually be Hessel. "Geeko" becomes unnerved while speaking to Harry, as he does not understand many of the idioms Harry is using. Harry says that he does not mean to be a "hassle," which "Geeko" mishears as "Hessel," thereby revealing his identity. Hessel escapes to a mountain, and Harry gives chase.

Choice line: "Listen, that routine about the clown with the painted smile and broken heart is so tired it squeaks." - Harry Lime

Intelligence check: Much like Mr. Arkadin, Hessel has never been photographed.

Comments: Another great episode in a mini-saga with Harry at the circus. The mine chase is a great exercise in sound design. Harry's narration to the audience echoes in the mine as he chases Hessel. The flashback structure was hard to follow at first, but necessary to show how differences in language, linguistics, and accents played into the downfall of Hessel. Radio is the perfect medium for a story so reliant on linguistic misunderstanding. Harry's continued insistence on calling Hessel by his circus name "Geeko" is a great way of robbing Hessel of any power he has. The Nazi is continually made into a fool.

The Lives of Harry Lime
Episode 40, "Suzie's Cue"
Original transmission: May 2, 1952
Listened to on June 18, 2017
Source: Internet Archive

Summary: After a brief start in Venice, Harry makes his way to Paris. By chance, Harry sees a newspaper story about the end of a trail regarding a necklace valued at $100,000. Harry brings in a few people to help him steal the necklace; of course, things don't quite work out for him.

Comments: blah blah blah stolen jewels blah blah blah loveliest woman ever blah blah double cross blah blah marriage blah blah blah

Seriously though, I did not like this episode. There's nothing specifically bad about the writing, but every trope that makes up the episode is something that's been done before many times in the series.

The Lives of Harry Lime
Episode 41, "Vive le Chance"
Original transmission: May 9, 1952
Listened to on June 18, 2017
Source: Internet Archive

Summary: Back to Paris. Harry is approached by two men, Paul and Pierre, to back them as they con a rich American named Witherspoon. Lizette, a friend to Paul and Pierre, tells Harry about her family's fortune that was lost during the Franco-Prussian War. She recently came across a letter that tells of a false bottom in a jewel case that has a map that leads to a family treasure. The case was lost, but was tracked to an area flea market. They need 5,000 francs in order to buy back the case. Returning to the market, the price of the case goes up to 2 million francs. Harry and Witherspoon both front 1 million francs to buy the case. They eventually get the case, but the dig results are disappointing.

Comments: Good story, but as the series begins to wind down, I have to acknowledge that double-crosses like these get enervating. Sure, they're good for yarns that can be quickly written and produced, but with so many great episodes in the series, this episode is a weak entry into the Lime canon.

The Lives of Harry Lime
Episode 42, "The Elusive Vermeer"
Original transmission: May 16, 1952
Listened to on June 20, 2017
Source: Internet Archive

Summary: At Cannes, Harry meets Horace St. John Wyndemere, a thief who specializes in breaking and entering. Wyndemere had just robbed the house of Lord

Brixton. While many valuables were stolen, the main attraction is an original (unidentified) Johannes Vermeer painting. Knowing the painting will be hardest item to get rid of, Wyndemere tasks Harry with its sale. Harry heads to London. He finds an American oil man who would like to buy the Vermeer for $150,000 in order to one-up a competing oil man who just bought an original Rembrandt. As Harry is about ready to make the deal, he discovers that Wyndemere has been murdered and the Vermeer sold to a pawn shop. Harry tracks the Vermeer painting through London.

Choice dialogue:

Wyndemere: I'll take a quick butcher's.
Lime: Uh, "butcher's"?
Wyndemere: Butcher's! A good look! Don't you understand English?

Comments: Considering the over-utilized tropes in the series, I was ready to hate this episode. There are still parts I am not exactly fond of, but I like how the episode wrapped up. So many people fake their death in this series that it was a shock that Horace actually *was* dead. While Harry has been foiled many times and Harry has been able to claim various rewards, the fact that Inspector Jones literally cited the $150,000 figure for the Vermeer is interesting on its own. While it could be argued that the ending feels tacked on, there are other things to consider: how did Harry know Jones? Did Hoffman rat out Harry before his own sale? Did Horace actually die? The ending isn't quite wrapped up, but it works here.

Above: "Lady Standing at a Virginal," by Johannes
Vermeer. One of the two "Lady at the Virginals" paintings
at the National Gallery, London, England.

The Lives of Harry Lime
Episode 43, "Murder on the Riviera"
Original transmission: May 23, 1952
Listened to on June 22, 2017
Source: Internet Archive

Summary: Côte d'Azur, 1946. Harry is smuggling American cigarettes in packages of powdered milk. Early one morning, Harry drives by a woman trying to push a limousine. In the limousine is a dead man. Harry goes to get the girl, whose name is Danielle. They head to Harry's apartment in Nice. Upon arrival, they find Lilly, one of Harry's old flames, in the apartment. Danielle says she needs to get back to her hotel in Paris, which has all of her important items. She further states that she had no idea who the man in the limousine was. Harry accepts the mission and takes his smuggling van, which is still filled with smuggled cigarettes. Lilly ends up tagging along. Arriving at the hotel, Harry breaks into Danielle's room. As he is about to leave, Harry comes across a picture that clearly shows that Danielle knew the dead man. Further, police have surrounded the cigarette van. Harry tries to escape and return to Nice.

Intelligence check: Harry, like Guy Van Stratten in *Mr. Arkadin*, is a cigarette smuggler in this episode.

Comments: Great, but I wonder why the episode ended with a wounded Harry that is about to be charged with major crimes. How is he going to get out of this? What is the resolution?

One recurring element of the series that I will never tire of is a foot chase, which are consistently well done.

On a simpler note, the image of Harry in his big coat and

hat is such a strong image from *The Third Man* that just hearing about him in shirt sleeves was a shock.

Other notes: The Internet Archive recording is far cleaner than the one on the Criterion Collection *Mr. Arkadin* set.

The Lives of Harry Lime
Episode 44, "Pearls of Bohemia"
Original transmission: May 30, 1952
Listened to on June 23, 2017
Source: Internet Archive

Summary: In Milan, Harry answers a newspaper advertisement to become a bodyguard and agent for aspiring beauty queen Melody Johnson. They set sail for a beauty contest in Cairo. While on the boat, Harry and Melody are followed by an unknown figure. They find that their cabin has also been raided. Melody reveals that she has a pearl necklace that once belonged to the Count of Bohemia. A man named Ziki is looking to regain the pearls after losing them to Melody while gambling on the French Riviera.

Comments: Good, but not a specifically great episode. I don't have much to say beyond that; I suppose I just feel ambivalent about it. This is especially true as it has just about the same ending as Guy de Maupassant's "The Necklace."

The Lives of Harry Lime
Episode 45, "A Night in a Harem"
Original transmission: June 6, 1952
Listened to on June 24, 2017
Source: Internet Archive

Summary: Between Paris, Zurich, Istanbul, and elsewhere,

Harry becomes privy to an island that is allegedly about to become the biggest source of oil in the Middle East. A cadre of people descends on the island to try and make their claim.

Comments: If the summary I provided seems vague, it is because any attempts at being specific would mean writing out the entire plot. The episode is ambitious, but the plot became convoluted with a surplus of characters and an over-complicated plot. "Dead Candidate" and even "Love Affair" did a lot of the same things but with better pacing. This episode tried to stuff two hours of material into a quarter of the time and suffered for it.

The Lives of Harry Lime
Episode 46, "Blackmail is a Nasty Word"
Original transmission: June 13, 1952
Listened to on June 24, 2017
Source: ***Mr. Arkadin*, Criterion Collection DVD**

Summary: Marseilles, 4 am, September 12, 1947. Harry is returning to his yacht when he is suddenly visited by a wounded man. The man has been stabbed above the heart. The man tells Harry that his name is Bracco, but wishes to be called Marcel as he passes away. Bracco says he was the chief of an all-female criminal group called The Amazons. Before he dies, Bracco gives Harry the name Maurice Chivret. Chivret is a deputy for the National Assembly of France and may have criminal connections. Months later, Harry speaks with Julian Moreau, a journalist and an acquaintance of his. Harry asks Moreau about Chivret and Bracco and finds out that the two are connected through The Amazons. Months after this meeting, a woman named Heidi asks Harry to help get her father out of Romania. Smuggling her father out would be too risky, but Harry knows the perfect person to blackmail in order to get

Heidi's father out of Romania diplomatically.

Choice line: "Honey, I'm always in trouble with the French police." - Harry Lime

Intelligence check: Harry is once again smuggling cigarettes. Bracco's arrival at the dock would later be adapted into *Mr. Arkadin*; although, the police are not pursuing Bracco in the episode.

Comments: Very good episode. I don't really sympathize with a dead Nazi collaborator, but the pacing was perfect to help unnerve Chivret. The two seemingly disparate plots worked very well together and this was a unique scrape for Harry to work his way out of.

The Lives of Harry Lime
Episode 47, "The Professor Regrets"
Original transmission: June 20, 1952
Listened to on June 24, 2017
Source: Internet Archive

Summary: Harry is at an unnamed casino off the coast of the Mediterranean playing Chemin-de-fer. He is playing against a Greek syndicate when he meets another beautiful woman. Harry invites her to the yacht he is looking after on behalf of Enrico de Sade. The woman is sharing a villa with a physicist named Hans. Hans is working on a project similar to the H-Bomb. Hans has been properly vetted to work on the project, but there are suspicions that he is trading secrets. Harry sets out to investigate.

Comments: I feel like this is supposed to be a riff on the then-ongoing Julius and Ethel Rosenberg trial. Paradoxically, there is a total lack of tension in the proceedings. It even ends on a weak note. Harry starts the story by saying he isn't the hero of the story; additionally, he neither wins nor loses.

The Lives of Harry Lime
Episode 48, "The Hard Way"
Original transmission: June 27, 1952
Listened to on June 24, 2017
Source: Internet Archive

Summary: Harry is in France, where his friend Moe is trying to get him to go legit. Times have changed and it is necessary to go toward a more law-abiding lifestyle. Harry accepts the idea, and Moe suggests that they run a private air charter company with an old, beat up plane they have. Harry reluctantly accepts the job. However, Harry is still under suspicion by local police, who have a dossier of his crimes going back to 1946. Harry says that Safeways Plane Charter, Inc. is a legit business, but is still under watch. A problem arises at the airport right before Harry's first charter. Soon, Harry finds himself in the midst of an illicit charter that could spell trouble for his new life.

Harry's past: Harry knows how to fly a plane.

Shakespeare: Referring to the age and condition of the plane Harry and Moe own, Harry says that it has seen "the chimes at midnight."

Comments: It could drag for at times, but Harry's attempt to go legit is worth a notice. As fresh and idea that is, Harry sticking around in France can be a little boring. Then again, as an English production, it would be easier to do episodes in France and other western European countries as opposed to other places around the world without having a wholly offensive accent.

The Lives of Harry Lime
Episode 49, "Paris is Not the Same"
Written by Joseph Cochran (Welles, et al 69)
Original transmission: July 4, 1952
Listened to on June 25, 2017
Source: Internet Archive

Summary: Back to Paris; specifically, Harry is on the Geneva Express and would rather be with anyone else than Duval, his train car companion. Duval is especially proud of his wife and Harry becomes smitten with her. Harry visits her and gets friendly with their butler Andre. Andre has black market connections to which Harry wishes to team up. Harry finds out that Duval is a maker of popular perfumes. Harry and Andre decide to hold up one of Duval's trucks, steal the perfume, and sell diluted versions of it on the black market to American soldiers. The soldiers send the perfume to their girlfriends at home, but since they don't know what Duval's perfume really smells like, there is no way to know it is a fraud. Eventually Duval finds out about the scheme.

Theme song: Harry whistles "The *Third Man* Theme" multiple times in the episode. He also professes to prefer zither music.

Harry's past: Harry may have attended and almost graduated medical school.

Comments: Cochran really forced as many *Third Man* references as he could into the episode, especially when Harry makes frequent mention of a "third man" at the head of the whole operation. That idea remains undeveloped, though it may just be Harry being tricky. Then again, the scheme does work as an early version of the one that would ultimately lead to Harry's demise.

The Lives of Harry Lime
Episode 50, "Honeymoon"
Original transmission: July 11, 1952
Listened to on June 25, 2017
Source: Internet Archive

Summary: In Sicily, Harry runs into a Hungarian countess named Cathy. He knows her from many of the rackets she tried in the past. When they meet, Harry finds out that she is working for *Blink*, a picture magazine. Cathy is trying to get images of alleged gangsters for a photo series and is hoping to get images of Plucky Mariello. Having recently met with Plucky, Harry assists Cathy. However, a murderer is on the loose and looking for Plucky, which leads to a confrontation at Plucky's. Cathy eventually gets her pictures, but she may not be able to keep them for long.

Choice line: "All technicolor and cast iron." - Harry, referring to Cathy

Comments: If the summary sounds awkward, it is because the first half is a solid adventure that had an ending, but everything falls apart in the second half. The bribe totally works at first, but the second half of the episode gets too convoluted for its own good.

The Lives of Harry Lime
Episode 51, "The Blue Caribou"
Original transmission: July 11, 1952
Listened to on June 25, 2017
Source: Internet Archive

Summary: Harry is in San Marino when he is visited by a palm reader. The reader tells Harry that he will be looking into something called the "Blue Caribou" in the near future. Harry knows this, as he was contacted about it earlier in the

66

day by Jennifer Chase. The Blue Caribou is a valuable piece of antique pottery that Jennifer recently purchased but was promptly stolen from her. Harry takes on the investigation, but finds out that the seller of the Blue Caribou may have had a hand in its robbery.

Theme song and more: Harry hums "The *Third Man* Theme" before Pietro attacks. Additionally, at one point Harry refers to Pietro as "Rosebud."

Comments: Good episode, but a wholly bizarre and out-of-place introduction. The added mysticism is quickly dismissed and never referenced again.

The Lives of Harry Lime
Episode 52, "Greek Meets Greek" (last episode)
Original transmission: July 25, 1952
Listened to on June 25, 2017
Source: Internet Archive

Summary: In Greece, a doctor concludes that Harry has measles and is quarantined to his room. Harry does not take this lightly. As he is officially put into quarantine, a woman named Andrea comes in and says that she needs to hide out in Harry's room. Harry is not interested, but Andrea insists. Going to her room to retrieve a few items, Harry plainly sees a dead man in the room. Andrea eventually confesses that she has been cheating on her husband. In turn, the husband is in the area hunting Andrea and the man she is with.

Attribution: In Jonathan Rosenbaum's timeline of Welles' works in *This is Orson Welles*, Welles is credited as writer on this episode (408). However, the "Greek Meets Greek" episode he mentions in the timeline is supposed to be a story source for *Mr. Arkadin*. Since nothing in this episode is particularly connected to *Mr. Arkadin*, it is likely the episode he mentions is an alternate title for another episode. Therefore, I have not put Welles name as the credited writer for this episode.

Comments: Solid premise that kept Harry in his room fell apart quickly. Andrea's hesitation to tell Harry *anything* made the story hard to get into. I was as annoyed as Harry was with the lack of information to work with. I'm perfectly fine with a MacGuffin, but with no actual art thievery, the final deal that Harry went for is too vague to be interesting.

Above: Joseph Cotten publicity image, circa 1957.

The Third Man
Source: *The Third Man*, Criterion Collection DVD (2007 reissue)
Directed by Carol Reed
Written by Graham Greene
Starring: Joseph Cotten, Valli, Orson Welles, Bernard Lee, Trevor Howard, Wilfrid Hyde-White, Ernst Deutsch, Erich Ponto, Siegfried Breuer, Paul Hörbiger
Viewed: July 3, 2017

Summary: American novelist Holly Martins is summoned to Vienna at the request of his friend, Harry Lime. Upon arrival, Martins discovers that Lime has been killed in a car accident. Holly eventually discovers there are more forces in play behind Harry's presumed death, and many people want to see Harry taken down.

Choice dialogue: The whole screenplay.

Harry's past: Holly says that he last saw Harry in September of 1939. In the timeline of the radio series, this would put their last meeting sometime after the events of "The Bohemian Star."

Comments: I've seen *The Third Man* many times, but this viewing took on a different air after the entire *Lives of Harry Lime* series. There was a little bit of shock that I would be following a Harry Lime story that wasn't narrated by Lime himself. I'm so used to Lime being a charming con man that I nearly forgot that he can be truly rotten. The already potent hospital scene becomes even harder to watch because of this.

Other notes: As I listened to the *Harry Lime* radio series, I was always struck by the fact that the announcer always referred to Harry Lime as an "immortal character" in the opening narration. This is in spite of the fact that Harry is dead by the time the series began. Then again, "immortal" may be used to describe Lime's popularity after death.

Above: Orson Welles, Rita Hayworth, and Joseph Cotten after the marriage of Welles and Hayworth.

Confidential Report
Version: Edited American version of *Mr. Arkadin*
Cast and crew same as the "Corinth" *Mr. Arkadin*
Source: The Complete *Mr. Arkadin*, Criterion
Collection DVD
Viewed: July 8, 2017

Comments: There are other books and articles analyzing the differences among the different versions of *Mr. Arkadin*. The sound and picture elements do appear to be better in this version. Whether one version of *Mr. Arkadin* is better than another is a matter of personal taste, there are artistic choices in *Confidential Report* that I like more than the "Corinth" version and vice versa. As my primary concern is *Mr. Arkadin*/*Confidential Report*'s connection to *The Lives of Harry Lime*, I'll avoid an exhaustive list of differences and focus on a cut line that I miss.

When Guy Van Stratten and Raina Arkadin reunite in Spain, Raina reveals that her father is Russian. Guy doesn't believe this and he brings up her father's amnesia. Just as Raina begins to laugh, the scene fades and cuts to Guy in Munich. In the "Corinth" version of *Mr. Arkadin*, the scene goes slightly longer, with Raina wrapping the conversation with, "Oh, really, chum. I never heard of amnesia lasting that long." In the original "Man of Mystery" episode, Raina further criticizes her father's amnesia, stating that she only knows of amnesia like that coming from "cheap books and bad movies."

I can understand getting rid of the "cheap books and bad movies" line from the final film. Arguably, it might hit too close to home. But the cut in *Confidential Report* comes off as sloppy. The original version fades from Raina's criticism to Van Stratten talking to Jacob Zouk before going on to Munich.

Most of all, I find it interesting to see how a line can evolve, or in this case devolve, from one version to another.

Above: *Mr. Arkadin* co-stars Paola Mori and Orson Welles, 1955.

The Lives of Harry Lime – **Numbers, Lists, and Stray Observations**

My Top 10 Episodes (in no particular order)

1. "Dead Candidate"
2. "Man of Mystery"
3. "Art is Long and Lime is Fleeting"
4. "The Painted Smile"
5. "Harry Lime Joins the Circus"
6. "A Ticket to Tangier"
7. "Too Many Crooks"
8. "Double Double Cross"
9. "An Old Moorish Custom"
10. "Work of Art"

Weakest episode: "Every Frame has a Silver Lining"

Stories featuring Harry in Paris: Ten

Stories set in Vienna, pre-*Third Man*: Two ("Love Affair" and "Man of Mystery")

Country never visited: Brazil. Considering the fact that Lime was taken to many countries and cities of real interest to Welles, I was really holding out for an episode taking place in Brazil. Because Welles was so fond of Brazil after filming *It's All True* in the early forties, I really felt like a Lime adventure would take him back there.

Currencies spent by Harry:
- American dollars
- Mexican pesos
- English pounds
- French francs
- Hungarian pengoes

Orphaned title: The title "Casino Royale" appears in Jonathan Rosenbaum's timeline of Welles' career in *This is Orson Welles* (408). However, it is not immediately apparent which episode this could be an alternate title for. There are episodes that take place in casinos, but I cannot confidently assign the "Casino Royale" title to any of them.

Potential chronology:

There is no established chronology to *The Lives of Harry Lime*. To put it another way, Harry doesn't narrate his adventures in the order they happened in his lifetime. The series had more in common with Sir Arthur Conan Doyle's original Sherlock Holmes stories, in that Watson narrated a story from any given point in his time with Holmes. However, there are a few episodes with explicitly stated years. Therefore, the following list is a potential chronology of stories from the radio series. Episodes without years have not been included. *The Third Man* is on the list to provide a finale for Harry Lime.

- 1936, "Double Double Cross" (Episode 25)
- 1937, "The Third Woman" (Episode 19)
- 1938, "The Bohemian Star" (Episode 6)
- 1942, "Clay Pigeon" (Episode 3)
- 1944, "Work of Art" (Episode 9)
- 1945, "In Pursuit of a Ghost" (Episode 16)
- 1946, "Murder on the Riviera" (Episode 43)
- 1947, "Blackmail is a Nasty Word" (Episode 46)
- 1947, "Man of Mystery" (Episode 37)
- 1949, *The Third Man*

Harry Lime and Holly Martins – Versions

Further versions of *The Third Man* and Harry Lime exist in radio and television. *The Third Man* was adapted for radio on three separate occasions. Additionally, *The Third Man* became the title of a television series featuring Harry Lime on a variety of adventures.

The year 1951 was a prolific for both Harry Lime and *The Third Man*. Before *The Lives of Harry Lime* came to radio that August, two adaptations of *The Third Man* would be produced by two separate radio series.

Theater Guild on the Air produced the first radio adaptation of *The Third Man,* which aired on January 7, 1951. Joseph Cotten reprised his role as Holly Martins. Signe Hasso inherited the role of Anna Schmidt. This adaptation retains much of the original story with little left out. Missing in this version of *The Third Man* is Harry's cuckoo clock speech. Harry's "dots" speech is also slightly modified. This time, Harry offers only $1,000 per dot as opposed to the $20,000 per dot in the original film. The zither score is also maintained here.

On April 9, 1951, *Lux Radio Theater* broadcast an adaptation of *The Third Man*. Once again, Joseph Cotten starred as Holly Martins. Evelyn Keyes played Anna Schmidt, and Ted di Corsia took on the Harry Lime role. The *Lux* version would utilize the zither theme on occasion, but stuck with the more melodramatic orchestrations that were common in the series. As opposed to the *Theater Guild* version of *The Third Man*, *Lux* version kept the cuckoo clock speech and the original amount of $20,000 per dot. Martins' speech at the literary society is cut in the *Lux* version.

The Third Man would be performed on Lux Radio Theater once more on February 8, 1954, with Ray Milland filling in for Cotten.

The Third Man television series ran from 1959 to

1965 and starred Michael Rennie as Harry Lime. Accompanying Harry on these adventures was Bradford Webster, played by Jonathan Harris. Webster was a secretary for Lime during the series, keeping up Lime's social schedule. The series ran for 77 episodes.

Rennie is only Harry Lime by name in his *Third Man* TV series. His Lime is a business man who just so happens to have connections to the underworld. In the episode "A Little Knowledge," Webster shows Lime a front page news item announcing Lime's arrival in Madrid. Rennie's Lime seems unconcerned with the announcement. It would be hard to imagine Welles' Lime having the same reaction to this news.

The series also features a new and more elaborate rendition of the Anton Karas theme song, but that is where the similarities end.

Above: Ted di Corsia in *Vengeance Valley* (1951), the same year he played Harry Lime in the Lux Radio Theater's first production of *The Third Man*.

Above: Michael Rennie in 1958, shortly before playing
Harry Lime in the TV series *The Third Man*, which ran
from 1959 to 1965.

End Note: Good Night

This part of my journey with Harry, Holly, and Orson has reached its end, but the journey is far from being over.

There are papers at University of Texas-Austin that demand my attention. I anxiously await the *Third Man* TV scripts at the University of Michigan archives.

And there is still Vienna.

I hope this is an enjoyable book. Hopefully it inspires more listeners of *The Lives of Harry Lime*. If the episode entries repetitive, I hope it is understood that the episodes themselves could be repetitive. Many episodes were great and others could be a chore to listen to. If the tone was too informal, I hope that it will not reflect poorly on my larger book about Welles' commercials. That project has been formally in progress since 2015 and will continue for the foreseeable future. This book presented a chance to prepare for the next stage of the larger project, loosen up about the subject, and learn self-publishing.

I've had the itch to learn self-publishing for a long time and this book became my formal education in it. I'll know what to say the next time one of my English students asks how to publish their own works.

To wrap on a personal, potentially Wellesian note, thank you for reading this book and I hope you stick around for the big one.

Good night.

Works Cited

F for Fake. Orson Welles, dir. Orson Welles, Elmyr de Hory, Clifford Irving, Joseph Cotten, perf. Les Filmes de L'Astrophore, 1976. DVD.

Johnson, Erskine. "In Hollywood" *The Miami Daily News-Record* [Miami, OK], 19 December 1947, p. 14. *Newspapers.com*. Accessed 15 May 2017. Web.

Miller, Sigmund. "Art is Long and Lime is Fleeting." *The Lives of Harry Lime.* London: Pocket Books for *News of the World*, 1952. Print.

Towers, Harry Alan. "Reviving Harry Lime." Robert Fischer, interviewer. *Mr. Arkadin*. Criterion Collection, 2006. DVD.

Welles, Orson and Peter Bogdanovich. *This is Orson Welles*. Jonathan Rosenbaum, ed. New York: HarperPerennial, 1992. Print.

Welles, Orson, ct al. *The Lives of Harry Lime.* London: Pocket Books for *News of the World*, 1952. Print.

Photo Credits

The following photos are in the public domain and were found at Wikimedia Commons:

Cover image: Wiener Riesenrad, June 11, 2004. Photograph by Chris Dixon.

Page 1: Orson Welles, 1941. Unknown photographer, originally distributed by CBS Radio.

Page 10: Pompeii street, 2007. Photograph by Wikimedia Commons user Alago.

Page 14: Engraving of Henri Christophe by Blasius Höfel, 19th century.

Page 15: Images from Federal Theater Project production of *Macbeth*, 1936. Photographer unknown, from collection of Works Progress Administration photographs.

Page 30: Lithograph of Oruç Reis by Charles Etienne Pierre Motte, modeled after an illustration by Achille Devéria, date unknown.

Page 31: Image of Oruç Reis by Charles Farine, 1869.

Page 59: "Lady Standing at a Virginal" by Johannes Vermeer, circa 1670-1672.

Page 69: Joseph Cotten, 1957. Unknown photographer, originally distributed by NBC Television.

Page 73: Paola Mori and Orson Welles, 1955. Photographer unknown, originally published by the Associated Press, May 5, 1955 in *The Stars and Stripes* Europe, Mediterranean, and North Africa editions.

Page 79: Michael Rennie, 1958. Photographer unknown, originally distributed by CBS Television on June 2, 1958 to promote *Climax!*

The following images are screenshots from public domain films:

Page 41: Images of Joseph Cotten from *Too Much Johnson*

workprint, 1938. Paul Dunham, cinematographer.

Page 52: Image of Frédéric O'Brady from *Mr. Arkadin* trailer, 1955. Jean Bourgoin, cinematographer.

Page 53: Image of Robert Arden from *Mr. Arkadin* trailer, 1955. Jean Bourgoin, cinematographer.

Page 78: Cropped image of Ted di Corsia from *Vengeance Valley*, 1951. George J. Folsey, cinematographer.